THE BREAKUP OF MY FIRST MARRIAGE: Poetry By Bruce Weber

- A Single Volume, 104 pages.
- Trade Paperback, American contemporary poetry collection by a single author.

Contact Information:

http://www.roguepress.com

Design and layout by C. D. Johnson

Painting, Front Cover and Frontispiece:
Joanne Pagano Weber, *Seasons* - Collection Of The Artist

Painting Copyright © by Joanne Pagano Weber

ISBN: 0-9771550-9-9
ISBN13: 978-0-9771550-9-5

Published by Rogue Scholars Press
New York, NY - USA

The Breakup Of My First Marriage

Poetry by Bruce Weber

Published by Rogue Scholars Press
www.roguepress.com

To My Father Harry Weber (1916-1981)

Acknowledgments

I would like to thank publishers C. D. Johnson and Miriam Stanley of Rogue Scholars Press for their great support in making this book possible. Also to the many poets in my immediate circle in the area of New York (both downstate and upstate) who have served as a continual source of words, inspiration and support. I would also like to thank Eve Packer, Angelo Verga, Susan Hoover, and Steve Dalachinsky for their special support of this project.

Thanks, as well, to ABC NO RIO and the Sunday afternoon reading series, which has continued to help spark my writing.

I would also like to thank my wife, Joanne Pagano Weber, who always succeeds in encouraging and prodding me on as a writer; and my friend Brian Boyles for lending his eyes in carefully reading through the manuscript.

Bibliography

These Poems Are Not Pretty (Miami: Palmetto Press, 1992)
How The Poem Died (New York: Linear Arts, 1998)
The First Time I Had Sex With T. S. Eliot (New York: Venom Press, 2004)
Poetic Justice (New York: Ikon Press, 2004)

Notation:

Some of these poems have appeared in *Stretching Panties*, *Witness*, *Tamarind*, *No Mad's Choir*, *11211*, *Longshot*, *Arts Society Of Kingston Calendar*, *Brownstone Poets Anthology*, *Stained Sheets*, and perhaps a few other publications the author has lost track of.

Table Of Contents

Table Of Contents continued...

Bruce Weber

Bruce Weber grew up in the East Flatbush section of Brooklyn in the golden age of New York baseball.

Over the past twenty odd years he has been active in the poetry scenes of New York and Florida.

He has long been involved with the alternative space, ABC NO RIO, and is the editor of the broadside **Stained Sheets**.

Since 1995, he has been the organizer of the *Alternative New York's Day Spoken Word / Performance Extravaganza*.

Weber's work has appeared in numerous magazines and publications including the anthologies **Up Is Up, But So Is Down: Downtown Writings, 1978-1992** (New York University, 2006) and **Riverrine: An Anthology Of Hudson Valley Writers** (Codhill Press, 2007).

He has performed regularly in the tri-state area of New York, both alone and with his group, *Bruce Weber's No Chance Ensemble*, which incorporates poetry, theatre, music and dance, and has produced the CD, **Let's Dine Like Jack Johnson Tonight**.

An art historian and curator by day, he is currently Senior Curator at the *National Academy Museum*.

Previously Weber was Director of Research and Exhibitions at *Berry-Hill Galleries*, where he curated and authored numerous catalogs, among them, **The Heart Of The Matter: The Still Lifes Of Marsden Hartley**, **Chase Inside And Out: The Aesthetic Interiors Of William Merritt Chase**, and **The Apple Of America: The Apple In 19th Century American Art**.

Weber's is also the author of **Paintings Of New York, 1800-1950** (Pomegranate Books, 2005).

Weber and his wife, the painter and writer Joanne Pagano Weber currently split time between their homes in New York City and the Woodstock area in upstate New York.

The Surgery Of Reality

When it comes to giving, Bruce Weber gives 150%, both as a poet and a humanist. From his efforts at the legendary *Unorganicized* readings at ABC No Rio, to his on-going success as founder and producer of the *Alternative New Year's Day Spoken Word / Performance Extravaganza,* to his many jobs as editor of zines and anthologies - not to mention his "real life job" as an art historian and curator - Bruce Weber has untiringly worked for almost 20 years as a mover and shaker in the poetry scene of New York City.

The poems in this wonderful new volume tell stories of love, loss, tragedy, tenderness and comedy. Some are fraught with sorrow and others with sarcasm. Some are filled with frustrated, though harmless anger and others with innocence and isolation. These poem are about "wrapping *forever* into a ball and javelining it out to sea". These poems are honest and filled with irony and whimsy. They play with language, the foundations of language, and the language of language.

The overall concept of the writing in this his fifth book of poetry is that of talkative, chattery monologues with "Us" the "World" as center stage. At times, his almost irritating tone provokes pathos, agitation and angst with his odd or unusual nuances and quirky rhythmic delivery. They are like a strong wind blowing through! Tugging at our hearts, minds and souls, pulling at our thoughts and scattering them around like leaves, while simultaneously unifying them in a pile to burn with passion and make us THINK!

Weber's always searching for what makes people tick. He portrays his adversaries as time bombs ready to explode at any moment.

For Weber, whose father passed away in 1981, and to whom this book is dedicated, the thread - the very heart of this volume - is FAMILY, real, imagined, collective, as well as universal and personal.

So if the cat got your tongue, I'm sure it'll loosen after reading this collection by this all-too-human being and his very, very humane voice.

- Steve Dalachinksy, NYC, June 2009.

and then he was dead

for Marc Desmond

yeah then he was gone. nobody missed him. except of course for the poets. but the poets miss everything. poets carry around the dead like necklaces or bracelets or talismans. fold the dead neatly into poems beside the few measly dollars in their wallet. and write odes or epitaphs or sweet little quatrains to how much a part of the world he was. because poets are you know. part of everything. cosmic creatures of a most peculiar sort. humming schubert while rhyming impossible words together. but then of course he was dead. there was no denying the heart attack in new york's most beloved bookstore on a frigid day in winter. he had probably just bought the newest translation of rimbaud and was going to have a café o lait at the corner before awaiting the next reading at the tavern off 14th street. first he'd stumble confusing his feet with the barricades of the french revolution and find a place looking out on the cavalcade heading down broadway like the world was on a conveyor belt on fast forward. he'd pull out his pen and write a poem and dunk a donut or two smiling in amusement at the world passing by his jaundiced eye in love with every crack in its armor every phosphorescent twinkle every bite into eve's apple every delicious word just sitting on his tongue like a new year's streamer awaiting a breath of cool air to jettison his imagination up to the moon and stars.

Bruce Weber

do's and don'ts

1) never siphon by mouth

2) always defer to your psychiatrist
    when he wants to harp on his neurosis

3) before going to the office remember
    to wipe down the rubber bed sheets

4) oppose any initiation rights to the van gogh fan club
    demanding the removal of your ear

5) concede defeat when confronted with
    the blood smeared pages of your journal

6) query your closest friends about which animals
    are too cute to eat

7) grab each pebble on the road and tell it you love it

8) regard each day as another chance to prove your mother wrong

i want my daddy

wah
wah
I want my daddy
wahhhhhhhhhhhhhh
wahhhhhhhhhhhh
I want my daddy
wahhhhh
wahhhh
where
did
my
daddy
go
?
where
is
my
daddy
hiding?
wah
wah
I want my daddy
I want him back home
wah
wahhhhhhhhhh
don't come near me
or
I'll
bite
you
I'll
spit
on
you
I'll
call
you
bad

names
wah
wahhhhh
wahhhhhhhhhhh
I want my daddy
wahh
wahh
I want my daddy
give
me
my
daddy
wah
wahhhh
you
you
you
wah
wahhhhh
wahhhhhhhhh
you
you
you
wah
wahhhh
I
miss
my
daddy
I
miss
my
daddy
why doesn't he come home?
wah
wah
wah
I
love

my
daddy
and
my
daddy
loves
me
wah
wahhhh
come
on
give
him
back
wah
wahhh
send
him
back
home
wah
wahhhhhhh
wahhhhhhhhhhh
I want my daddy
wah
wahhhhhhh
wahhhhhhhhh
I want my daddy
why
did
my
daddy
leave
me
all
alone
?

Bruce Weber

untitled poem for the twin towers

1.

the world is no longer as simple as a b c says the news commentator on tv. is he paraphrasing lincoln or helen of troy or woodrow wilson or marie antoinette or fdr or constantine or joan of arc? is he hiding history in a steamer trunk on the 110th floor of a skyscraper no longer with us? is he erasing ghengis khan from history's memory bank with merlin's magic wand? is he stumbling like a seasick passenger upon the sinking lusitania?

2.

good morning city. another day of digging. wrapping. numbering. dna-ing. another day of not surrendering. of raising a flag. of persisting. of never saying die. another day of repeating a mantra. of not jogging in place. of meditating on a flower. of reciting a poem by li po. about forever. about wrapping forever into a ball. about wrapping forever into a ball and javelinning it out to sea. the beautiful beautiful sea.

3.

mike told me about chet stanley last night. horrible. mr. stanley was trapped on the 92nd floor. his head was wedged between fallen debris. didn't want to hear it. entered a kind of "numb" zone. nothing there. except air and light and white noise. clung to this kind of embryonic state like a fish sucking up air. like i was back in the womb. like my skin was invulnerable to any kind of attack. closed my eyes. swooned there. drifting off like fog. across the mighty hudson. across to jersey. across to the inner continent where everyone raises a drink to the courage of fighter fighters and police. felt proud to be an american. like i was in a time warp. like i had watched too many episodes of "this was world war two". excused myself. slipped out into the sooty air. coughed till i fell unconscious. dreamed none of this happened.

a strong wind

a strong wind is blowing through this town.
pulling laundry off the line. upturning
garbage cans. lifting lawn furniture across
the yard. the wind swirls the leaves off trees.
pushing them around like naughty children.
tears off limbs and rocks the hammock
back and forth like a ghost's having a
hearty laugh on its account. this wind lifts
the skirts of women walking along the road.
it tempts the habits of the nuns praying for
the poor at the soup kitchen on main street.
it sizzles through the air like a guided missile
taking off for parts unknown. i wish the
wind would admit its nervous discontent /
struggle with the grip of its problems / and
count to ten without ever blowing its top.
confide its symbolism. the weight of its
meaning on a silver platter. dressed up
with a sprig of parsley. tied in red ribbon.
defined. classified. and laboratory tested.
sit down with the wind. dry its head off.
wipe the sweat from its forehead. listen to
the wind. learn from the wind. become the
winds deepest ally. the wind's most intimate
friend. and then the wind will call it a day.
the wind will give up its wars. the wind will
sleep quietly in our arms.

the thick and thin of the poem

this is the story.
oops.
this is the poem.
do not want to make a mistake.
no.
this is the poem.
you can tell because it
narrows
becoming
thin
as
a
word
p
a
s
s
e
d
between spokes in a fence.
a poem does not require much
an ear
a listening ear
a deeply listening ear
no
a casual ear
casual as this poem slipping from my typing fingers
no struggles over the fit of syllables
no adjustments to meter
assonance
dissonance
strophe
hah!
no
a poem demands a listening ear
a closely listening ear
glued to the page
requiring the surgery of reality for removal

the poem humorless
as
the society of american poets
holding the reins of tradition
with a pitchfork up their arse!
no
only kidding
yes only kidding
now back to this story
oops
ahem
this poem
this sweet sweet poem
sweet as orange marmalade
stickying the hands of schoolboys
gooing up the pages of the poems of yeats
blessed yeats
a first edition of yeats
o
my
god
a first edition of yeats ruined
o
merde!
now let me tell a story
a story long as an epic poem about gilgamesh
the long and short of it
the thick and thin of it
the tall and stout of it
little tea pot of a poem
little tug boat of a poem
fitting in your secret decoding ring's hatch
disappearing into the ether of unreality
dissolving under the tongue of the captured spy
the fading into absence spy
the dying spy
heroic as this poem
pinning medals to its epauletted shoulders
wearing itself out proudly in the world

like a poem
about the isle of innesfree
lovely isle of innesfree
spent a summer there one night
oops
spent a night there one summer
chasing yeats' ghost
around the lake
till i deeply understood symbolist poetry
the meaning of words clashing together like horns
in an archeologist's dictionary
like this poem
coded
secretive
pre-emptive
awaiting your angry retaliation
friend
comrade
fellow
lover of verse!
of poesy!
of the thick and thin
of
the
poem!
hallelujah
glory
hallelujah
glory
glory
hallelujah!

uhmm

m is a comfortable sound in my mouth. like marbles in the palm of a playful child. the smooth feeling of roundness. perfect roundness. m is the first letter of music. the most important letter in the word muscle. the raison d'etre for mimi and michael and michelle. m is never miserable and always mooing. m is moralistic as that fable about solomon your father told you while bouncing you upon his kneecap. m is mirthful and mercurious. m is never mendacious like the letter o or p or q. m sits and meditates on the rock in the buddhist garden. losing the mundane world. embracing the meaning of nothingness. the lock stock and barrel of the moon. the grand old moon up their in the marvelous midnight sky.

Bruce Weber

the adventures of lassie

as a boy i was a regular member of the sunday evening american television audience tuned in to the adventures of lassie. my face pressed within smelling distance of the black and white screen serving up an imaginary scenario starring lassie the wonder dog and her perfectly mannered rural american family breaking bread together in a plain as nails farmhouse. i wanted to work out a trade with god and become golden-locked blue-eyed deep-dimpled little timmy always deferring to the house rules of his beautiful mommy and daddy. whose grainy voices never rose far above a whisper in some perfect heartland setting, a million starry miles from the reality of my brick lined neighborhood in brooklyn, where emotion smashed its fists on the dinner table. i wanted lassie as a bodyguard in my daily peregrinations with the reality of the school yard, to tackle the bully of the neighborhood, to save me from accidental slips into manhole's, to shield me from the bickering conversation of my parents over the rising cost of my hand-me-down clothes. i wanted to climb inside the small rectangular screen and live with my big brainy dog, with the elegant thinness of katherine hepburn, the smooth as sugar glide of roger bannister, and the courage of a greek mythical hero daring medusa to eyeball 'em into stone.

tongue

huh?
cat got your tongue?
the heebee jeebies got your tongue?
come on baby show me your tongue
don't be shy
i've heard rumors about
your smooth as silk tongue
your whisper in a sow's ear tongue
your automatic retracting tongue
your long as a peg-legged sailor's tongue
your sweet as yam pie tongue
show it to me
i'll throw silver dollars
i'll promise to make the bogey man
step away from your bed
curl your tongue out like a red carpet
welcoming me into your mouth
like the arrival of jesus in jerusalem
like the touchdown of A grade a hurricane
offer your tongue
as a human sacrifice
to my inordinate hunger
my never able to be satisfied appetite
my let's walk the last mile attitude
for
your
banana
ripe
tongue
your
o
boy
here
it
comes
tongue
your
i

Bruce Weber

gotta
have
it
now
tongue
swirling around my mouth like a snake
doing its rhythm dance in my ionosphere
coming into the home stretch of my o my what a beautiful tongue

which williamsburg?

williamsburg. william carlos williams burg. o that's where that baby doctor poet lived? right? williams burgh. o no that's where edward hopper's from right? you know the one who painted scenes off the side of the turn of the century peeling away no matter what they do williamsburg bridge. hopper didn't move to brooklyn. pollock didn't move to brooklyn. but kline moved to brooklyn, right? williamsburg. where my daddy was from. he'd take me sunday shopping on the raggedy lovely streets of the lower east side then come back up with our car on the brooklyn homeboy side showing me the streets where his sixteen year old brother was murdered. where his father died of cancer at 42. you mean that williamsburg. the tenements now covered by projects side of williamsburg. the boyhood town of the american cubist painter max weber who grew up in a no longer existing by the j-train williamsburg. yo williamsburg. i know you. i can pick you out in a lineup. i can coax you into shaking your booty on the l, g or m line. i can indisputably prove you were that hot tamale on the dance floor that night in williamsburg. the one who went swimming in the alligator laden waters of that bar in williamsburg. the one sniffing up to the dames or gents or whatever in the bar of the charlestown williamsburg or the dead don't know the waterside sky at sunset on the hottest day of summer kind of williamsburg. o williamsburg artistes. o hasidic riddle of williamsburg. o benny. yeah. o benny. the williamsburg you rock to sleep every night in your arms. yeah. the williamsburg that dinah shore used to sing like a whisper in the ear of her lover. that williams burg. that's the williamsburg i mean.

Bruce Weber

the breakup of my first marriage

"this better be good", she said, "or i'm leaving"
and
when i read a poem
refuting suburban life
she left in an 80 mile an hour wind
with the trees, plants, hedges,
lawn furniture, grill, coasters,
crochet set, darts, deck of cards
and
tv
and
i was no longer welcome in my own home
the oriental carpet stared up at me
like a labyrinth
every pattern
introducing me to
another paradox
of cartesian equations
every electric light
dimmed on and off
threatening me
with their
perspicacity
the door swinging in my face
and knocking out my front teeth
because
the day she left
the refrigerator defrosted
drowning all my memories
they were floating in a fish tank
among kissing gouramis
and buck toothed piranhas
and the sink overflowed
causing all the bedbugs
to pack up and move
i wanted to scream something
that would make her stay
but all i could think of

were reruns of the
honeymooners
it was as if ralph cramden
finally realized
what an asshole
he was
to alice
and
went to therapy
and came out
a perfectly adjusted
bus driver
suddenly it was as if my body
was pressed into a configuration
anticipating the arrival
of the first lady
but the house still treated me like a stranger
every mirror had a joke to tell
the toilet kept laughing unmercifully
tickling me every time i sat down
and the bed sheets kept trying to strangle me
until i nailed them to the mattress
and the only answer
was to shoot everything
with my 44 caliber pistol
and i kept emptying bullets
and telling my home to behave
until it was destroyed
then i moved out

Bruce Weber

by way of explanation

by way of explanation
i'm the gnat
who got stuck
under the tongue
of mahatma gandhi.
by way of explanation
i'm easily confused
about where to put my mouth
during foreplay.
by way of explanation
i'm the gyroscope
who can't stop spinning.
by way of explanation
i'm the kid in the back row picking his nose
and flinging it out the window.
by way of explanation
i'm stumbling to the finish line of a race
i've absolutely no chance of winning.
by way of explanation
i need to know what's worth fighting for
and what i'm capable of losing.
by way of explanation
i'm leaving.
i'm missing.
i've never even been here.

who's dick is charles simic sucking?

who's dick is charles simic sucking?
can you tell me so i can get my poems
published regularly in the *new yorker*?
please point me in the right direction
and i'll do whatever's required
to penetrate that literary fortress
on west 43rd street
so i'll be considered a legitimate player
on the contemporary poetry circuit
i'll swallow down anything i have to
without even fluttering an eyelash
cause when my poems appear in the *new yorker*
i can give up being a third class artist
squirreling around for a two bit reading
in order to get my measly ten minutes
before a meager audience
on some sort of medication
yeah everybody'll commute
to manhattan from the suburbs
to a buy a 50 dollar ticket
to the 92nd street y
to kneel at the feet of my poems
and my mother
finally will stop berating me
for wasting my life
on something that'll never
make me any money
yeah so who's dick do i gotta suck
to get my poems published
on the slippery pages
of the *new yorker*?

Bruce Weber

without candles

for Abbie Hoffman

it was too late,
too cold,
too frightening
to drink the water,
to bathe,
to maneuver
in the bushes
among the trees,
no one knew,
because
no one understood
the rise of leukemia
in small towns,
children covered
with blue abrasions,
holes the size of quarters
in their sides,
blood and intestines dripping
staining the sheets,
feeding the worms,
the leeches,
the babies on fire,
burning from the chemicals,
the sun too pale to penetrate
their wounds,
their aches,
to warm their milk,
fertilize their brain,
the spurs,
the thorns,
the prickly roots,
the spiky branches,
the arms of the tree
embracing,
gripping the human heart
and the rot of babies

born to waste,
to hunger,
to die of thirst,
of civil wars,
civil disobedience,
civil unrest,
in the dark
utopia

Bruce Weber

blue flower

last
night
i
dreamt
i
brought
you
this
blue
flower
here
it
is
just
for
you
this
blue
flower
i
brought
from
my
dream

little jimmy

little jimmy sticks his tongue out at me like he's a lizard, drawing it in and out of his mouth like he's the fastest draw in a hollywood western, and little jimmy pretends to be a helicopter blade, swinging his arms and nearly cutting off my head, that's when billy puts a pail of red ants on his stomach, and fixes a scalding bath and keeps pushing little jimmy back in, when he's stamping his feet and kicking, and aunt wilhelmina used to rock little jimmy in her arms, humming melodies about the devil's work and throw him up in the air like he was a pillow, letting him almost fall to the ground, then grabbing him inches off the earth because she said it would help him to be balanced, and sometimes little jimmy shuts all the lights in the house, and little jimmy climbs my body like i'm a mountain, and little jimmy holds my waist like i'm some kind of anchor, like i'm in tune with some strange melody inside his head, making him purr, making him cackle, making him sleep with his little head on my shoulder.

Bruce Weber

payback

it's
time
you
give
me
some
passionate
payback
for my dog-like loyalty
before your tinsel-tipped pasties
before your shimmering eyelashes
before your spiked-boot heels
leading me
to your dressing room
for some extracurricular
x-rated action
because
i deserve to be treated extra special
for coming
to your strip show
for 100 straight nights
and feeding you abraham lincoln's
for shaking your booty
within inches of my gaping eyeballs
for making me sweat like a human waterfall
whenever you squat over my face
so i can get a whiff of your odiferous juices
so
go
ahead
apprize me of your appreciation
for my dog-like loyalty
throw me a silk stocking
throw me a garter belt
throw me a piece of your sleazy costume jewelry
and i'll gather your trinkets
in a museum dedicated to your beauty
because

you glitter up my sad-sack life
sticking your titties
within licking reach
of my tongue
making my penis wag
like a blind man's cane
tapping wildly on the sidewalk
lighting up my depraved imagination
like a ghetto child
setting off a row of firecrackers
igniting my body
like a human rocket
rattling
and
rolling
my
fevered
soul
to
armageddon

Bruce Weber

july 6th

for LD

the divorce was final on july 6th.
it was a long day.
i went to the beach
and jumped in a wave.
i joined my oldest friend tommy
for a shot and a beer.
i went to the strip club
and lap danced with shirley.
i took a long walk over the bridge
and remembered the night we fell in love
and got all tangled up
in
wishes
that
never
come
true.
i drove to your street
and sat in the car
and hummed the song
i used to sing you to sleep.
i remembered all the times we made love when we first met.
i remembered all the times we held hands in the movies.
i remembered all the times we fought over the dirty dishes in the sink.
i remembered all the times we saved each other from ruin.
and
cried
and
cried
and
cried.
the divorce was final on july 6th.
it was a long day.

open mike

i
was
planning
to impress you
with a love poem
i wrote for
the
cockroaches
multiplying
in
my
filthy
little
dwelling.
i was going
to mesmerize you
with a haiku
about
the
gaping
holes
in
my
head.
i
was
considering
amusing
you
with a chapter
from my autobiography
recounting the times
i should have apologized
to my mother
for
misbehaving
with
the
kitchen
burners.

Bruce Weber

i
was
going
to
recite
something
i wrote this morning
on a couple of hundred napkins
but
i
accidentally blotched them
with
a
bowl
of
clam
chowder.
i
was
going
to
tell
you
about
the
commendation
i
received
from the mayor
for scaring away
a flock of hungry pigeons
from the carcass of an infant
splattered
across
broadway
by
a
cabbie
hurrying
home
to

face
mecca.
i
was
going
to
charm
you
with
a couple of hundred anecdotes
about
my
adolescent
battles
with
pimples.
i
was
going
to
demonstrate
the dozen voices
simultaneously holding conversations
in
my
head.
i know you're terribly disappointed
but
i'm
going
to
be
a
responsible
open-
miker
and
keep
this
short.

the woman with the big laugh

she has a laugh the size of a cannonball. when she expresses it
the whole room shakes in delight. that's why he married her.
twenty-seven and a fireman and a stake in danger and a good
pension and he'll inherit his parents' acreage and the money
that's been mounting up since his great grand daddy settled
in these parts when hope sprang eternal. her bright prospects
never dim or falter and her smile lights up the rickety old
trailer and gleams up the counters of the tiny kitchen and
shines the surface of the ramshackle floors that've seen better
days. sometimes love's contagious. it just gets caught on you
and you don't know what you're doing but your heart does and
a smile as wide as a river can cover up most uncertainties
and a good country song on the radio heals all rainy forecasts.
she'll be pregnant within a month. and he'll merit commendations
for rescuing folks that strayed too near the flames. time will
raise a toast to their young marriage here among the hills
and dales and promises of a better richer life in tune with
crying babies and broken pencil points and marks that rise
on a wall and the indisputable elegance of wisdom taking its
place in the line of fire of life and love and dreams never
coming true.

maybe

maybe
i'm a little bit lax
about important things
like betrayal
maybe
i should live
in my own mind
without any help
from psychedelics
maybe
i should sit still
cross my arms
and meditate on something
kind and gentle
like that doll
i had as a kid
who never
booed
or
hissed
or
told me
i was stupid
maybe
i should have
dimmed
the
house
lights
so no one
would have recognized
the thousand karat ring
i stole from tiffany's window
maybe
i should have
used my own name
instead of yours
when i signed

Bruce Weber

that silly confession
maybe
i should stop chasing
the idealized woman
in the illusionistic
ceiling painting
in the lobby
of my building
maybe
i was wrong
to have hidden you away
for so many years
in the basement closet
maybe
you should turn over
that summons
that court order
that writ of habeas corpus
and
accept
me
back
in your bedroom
maybe
i should have told you
a long time ago
that
i
love
you

the superintendent of this neighborhood

don cherry yeah don and me were two peas in a pod. back in those days don and charlie haden and ed blackwell and me were living on lower second avenue and hanging all night around the corner at the five spot playing tunes and ragging on each other till the sun turned cherry red. yeah - cherry red - that was the name of a tune we played on the blue note album *the breakdown*. ornette and thelonious and clifford and i were very tight in those days. when clifford came to town i introduced him to art blakey and that's how he got his first gigs. by the late '50s i got tired of making chump change so i gave up tinkling on the piano, you dig? it was a hell of a lot more profitable selling heroin to my buddies in the jazz scene. man, i felt like a million dollars because i was doing everyone a favor supplying what ever they needed to stimulate their sounds. miles would never have peeled off notes from his horn so slow and spacey and sensual. the jazz scene would've fallen flat on its rump without my help, you dig? we'd still be in the swing era listening to some clones of sidney bechet playing dance tunes on the clarinet. they say the history of jazz is a history of changes in rhythms and my stuff helped mellow it down. it was just a twist of fate i supplied the drugs which polished off charlie parker - he already looked like a dead man the night he came over for his last hit. all the musicians whose habits i fed have passed away. now i'm the most popular building superintendent in this neighborhood. i ought to be written up as a hero but my name ain't mentioned anywhere in the history of jazz. in my heyday man i was the most loved cat around.

Bruce Weber

the war ended

the war ended. and everyone was glad. very glad.
mucho glad. especially the revolutionaries raising
their glasses to the end of all autocratic governments
that should have known better. the war ended.
and everybody was happy. especially the children.
the children wiped the tears away from the eyes
of the widows and parents. the children placed
roses beside the crosses of the dead. the children
made colored drawings of seraphim's like they
were the offspring of william blake's imagination.
the war ended. and the world took a deep breath.
the world sighed. the world got on its knees and
thanked god who art in heaven.

sniff poem

i'm a prurient interest. sniff me. come into my cave. my casa. my cuckoo's nest. sniff around my enticing behavior. arousing the feline in you. the tigress. the euphrates. opening your flood gates to hell and high water. because you can't resist the pull of my ardor. whispering to your dark side. the one you hid in the naughty play rooms of your childhood. yes sniff around me. fill my palms with silver dollars. decorate me like i'm a pagan thrown to dionysus and his tiger skin clad clan of banshees. swallow me up like i'm a bottle of retsina. get high on my odor. high enough to blow your cover. high enough to parade down main street america wearing only mother nature's clothing. and i'll coo your name out loud in the sexy lairs of my imagination. come sniff me like i'm your savior / your christ / your lottery jackpot winner. giving in to your deepest subliminal urges. i'm wanting. i'm willing. i'm waiting.

he was desperate

his voice snarled
like a whip
about to snare a snake
out of the wild brush
in the louisiana panhandle.
and his voice was scratchy
like some record
played over and over again
on the victrola.
and
he growled like a tiger
and
lunged his hand out
lunged his hand out
lunged his hand out
like he was going to snap you in half
with his bare knuckles.
they took him to the hospital outside los angeles.
the one that was recently on the news.
the one that nearly burned to the ground
when an inmate
set fire to a pair of pajamas.
but he's fine.
just fine.
he says he was doing his daily calisthenics.
when the match was lit.
he says he was busy catching mosquitoes
when the fire spread
burning though the
sheets and furniture
and curtains.
he says he was looking up at the stars
when the hospital caught fire
at three o'clock in the afternoon.

poem swiveling on a dime

his life turned on a dime. oops. his life swiveled on a dime. no. his life swerved on a dime. better. more visual. yes. his life swerved on a dime. make it a quarter. his life swerved on a quarter. make it a half dollar. his life swerved on a half dollar. yes. he could go east or west and he went east. west's more accurate. his life swerved on a half dollar and he could go east or west. he went west. after that his life blossomed. oops. after that his life floundered. his life capsized. his life jetted downhill like an olympic cross country skier. a simile. wonderful. his life swerved on a half dollar. he could go east or west. he went west. after that his life jetted downhill like an olympic cross country skier. until he met mindy. oops. roberta. until he met roberta. the lap dancer at louie's in massapequa. the prostitute who worked the meat packing district. the thousand dollar a night call girl at 900-637-4652. oops. 900-633-4573. then his life turned east and he could smell the roses. the jasmine. the apple blossoms. every morning he opened his eyes and thought it's good to be alive. oops. every morning his eyes popped open and he thought ain't life swell. oops. every morning his eyes jumped open and he contemplated the pleasures of life. the aphrodisiac of life. the fragrances of life. no. every *matin* he opened his eyes and shook his head at the spectacle of life and death and the human skull lighting up like the fourth of july in the window of the voodoo priestess pontaine cherie. yes. pontaine cherie. the wonderful sexy pontaine cherie.

Bruce Weber

chaim soutine's hat

for Steve Dalachinksy

there's chaim soutine's hat
under a plexiglas vitrine
in the museum.
plain brown hat.
black band around the crown.
innocuous.
respectful of the norm
when hats were common garb
for the gentleman out on the town.
chaim soutine's hat?
quirky neurotic aquaphobic chaim soutine's hat?
messy fingerpaint thick painter
chaim soutine's hat?
impossible.
fictitious.
fraud!
isn't that a bourgeoisie hat
a common man's hat
not the hat worn by the man
who held dead chicken's up by the neck
and posed for photographs
proud of his prize
a
madman
among bellhops
and skipping children
and
the
torrential
landscape
of
cheret
the
fire
climbing
the

38

roads
the
mountains
the
clouds
no
that can not be chaim's hat.
there are no stains
of so much sweat
so much inertia
so much turbulence in the air
turning
and
turn
ing
in
the
acid
blue
sky
herrings
jangling
on
a
plate
so
much
wind
so
much
thunder
at
the
butcher
the
red
carcass
the
pasty

cook
winking
at
the
world
no
it's impossible
it's too tame
too sedate
no it should be twitching
like a bat locked in a closed room
no that can't be chaim soutine's hat

always

your work has structure she says
not like his. that stuff just wanders
everywhere. directionless. formless.
pandering to mirrors and illusions.
it's pornographic. lewd. insensitive.
taboo-like in its desire to offend.
your work sings in key. obeys the
currents of the wind. shakes its head
at impossible puzzles. bows before
implacable yearnings. celebrates
air fire water earth. your work has
pathos. restores my faith in apple
trees / mistletoe / sweet potato pie.
your work has a joie de vivre.
leaping over the shoulders of
the sacramental. the transcendent.
his work stumbles out of the gate.
sags in the middle. angrily shakes
its mane. your work never succumbs
to excessiveness. always
clips its nails. always rings in my
ears like the grand canyon.

Bruce Weber

poem for micki siegel dying at age 59 on a snowy day

the snow is falling
across the sky
of my window
drifting across the prairie of the street
like a ghost of micki's life
she ain't here to see the snow
she died this morning at 4 a.m.
and i'm wishing she could be here to see the snow
worship the snow in one of her poems
take the snow home on her back like a little child
play in the snow
her red hair all tangled up in white's confusion
white's bulky wetness
white's ever ready punch of a snowball
zooming across the sky like a javelin
no micki ain't here no more
unless she's that streak of snow
passing by my window
leaving a hint she's here
in the shadows
in the dust
in the reflections
in the moonbeams
micki
just
a
step
away
in our minds
in our poems
in our imagination's
the snow
there's micki
the moon
there's micki
the bright and luminous sky
that's micki

hi i'm marilyn monroe

hi.
i'm
marilyn.
yes beautiful beautiful marilyn.
you know.
the gal who died of an overdose of barbiturates.
don't be fooled by these pants
or this beard
or this cock.
beneath this calm masculine exterior
is marilyn monroe.
darling marilyn.
the dame who married jolting joe.
you see marilyn was reincarnated as me.
little me.
moi.
i found this out accidentally
while watching *diamonds are a girl's best friend* on tv.
what a wonderful movie.
i knew it instinctively.
that was me on screen
pretending not to recognize
tony curtis and jack lemmon
underneath their dresses.
wasn't that directed by billy wilder?
whatever happened to billy wilder?
is he one of those disinherited directors?
and elia kazan?
whatever happened to elia kazan?
anyway
i'm marilyn monroe.
if you don't believe it
you're stupid.
stupid. stupid. stupid.

Bruce Weber

the man in the ten thousand dollar gucci suit

he's a nice guy but he got thrown out of california and told to never come back you know that happens when you're young and he was only sixteen and deserved a fresh start so they cleared the slate in new york like he wasn't a punk or had any history of violence and he started wearing a white suit and tie with a stickpin and opened an art gallery downtown cause you don't need to know anything to sell art you can be a village idiot everybody knows that and he connected with his sicilian heritage so that he could put up the money with no problem and started buying shit for ludicrous prices at the auctions to make a name for himself and he was stuck on people's tongues who care for stuff like that and you know that's understandable he artificially pumped up the market and gave it an inflated life and in the short run that's good for everybody from the guy pouring glasses of water at the restaurant to the guy smoking a cuban cigar in tavern on the green and millionaires got on waiting lists to buy the new artists he was peddling because that happens in a capitalist economy and this guy was a master at greasing palms and the mob was happy cause he was bringing in truckloads of dough even when the recession hit he was the only one making a splash and putting out catalogues and getting first page treatment in the press and the buzz word was out on the streets that he must be money laundering for the mob and i was telling some cops i know that its good for america that some guinea comes out of the blue and doesn't know squat and couldn't tell you the difference between andy warhol and pablo picasso and sells every piece of shit he gets his hands on and i understand the feds arrested him last night because he was just hot air in a ten thousand dollar gucci suit masquerading like every piece of art's crème de la crème yeah i knew it was just a matter of time before the karma would come right back.

diary entry sept 8th

ran into blood on the avenue last night. informed me about the gash sally took in the head from her boyfriend stewy and how she had to make a visit to the emergency room. second time this week she had to do that. stewy's too big and ornery for any of us to handle. but blood and i talked about going into his apartment with our guns flying and putting our barrels up his nostrils and scaring the shit out of him. we're too chicken shit to do it though. down the street ran into myrtle and her girlfriend louise. they're a happy pair. louise seems nicer than when i first met her. myrtle's lucky. they're playing tomorrow night at ace's and thought it would be worth checking out. at louie's bumped into dirk and his pet cobra belinda. she's kind of cute but when she started hissing i almost jumped up on the bar. dirk said the effect of the poison only lasts a couple of painful hours. yeah right! over at the café noir met penny for a drink and a discussion of her manuscript about that psycho killer who terrorized the neighborhood ten years ago. quite an achievement even if she isn't able to list her sources. makes the son of sam seem like a choir boy.

you

you're an idiosyncrasy.
a fatal error message.
a blink at the end of a game
of russian roulette.
you're the shame after.
the reflection on sin in paul 13:7.
you're blasphemous
as that silly cartoon
on the walt disney channel
starring daisy duck as a harlot.
you're too big
to get in this poem
especially when i'm trying
to sneak it in my back pocket
on my way out of cuba.
you're forlorn
on valentine's day
counting petals
from a plastic daisy.
you're the guy
who promised
a deep return
on my investment
and disappeared forever
to guadalajara
or someplace
equally polysyllabic.
you're the stranger
who whisked little timmy off
in a paper bag
at the movies.
you're the righteous preacher
at the back of the dial
of the local radio station
gathering converts like flies
to the rump of a horse.
you're the brutal one
my sister clara re-enacts every night

in dreams
she wouldn't want to touch
with a misloaded pistol.
you're all of the above
plus
you easily get hysterical
especially
when you get dressed
for the evening
for your small role
as a palomino pony
in that silly little play you're an extra in
on off-off broadway.
actually i like you
i find you amusing
you tickle my fancy
you stir up my imagination
like a wild brush fire
you set off an alarm
in the deepest reaches
of my subconscious
emitting sparks
from my head
like angie's sister helena
who climbed aboard
a firecracker
on the fourth of july
and still's circling
the moons of pluto

Bruce Weber

lea

the little kitten investigates empty boxes, labyrinthian mazes of shoes and belts and ribbons, the perch of high places which impels her to meow. the little kitten is excited about the way light plays a rhythmic dance against the wall. filtered by the swinging curtain in the breeze. the implications of so much movement. the deeper meaning of what makes up the world. the little kitten is a modern age philosopher. wittgenstein with a tail. rodin's thinker with paw on chin deliberating on the chain of things falling in place one by one on a domino board. and when i hold her in my hands up to the sky/right side up/upside down/or the other way around she observes the nature of the obtuse/the diagonal way we move on skis/the arm becoming a shovel throwing her the ball. my little kitten completely enthralled by my forefinger rubbing below her chin soothing her inclination to be mischievous. and the little kitten purrs and spins on to her belly discovering the more loving ways of the world without putting up her paws to fight or pushing back at so much attention like she's a movie star pulling so many interesting things into her world like a ball of string coming apart mystifyingly in her tiny churning arms.

my mommy and daddy don't love me

my mommy and daddy don't love me
so
i'm gonna hide
underneath my bed
and
hold
my
breath
to
the
count
of
a
hundred
or run away to kansas
and find dorothy
and walk down the yellow brick road
with her
and her little dog toto
my mommy and daddy
won't let me have a pet
they say animals smell bad
and i say how about goldfish
and they laugh
and hit me with a ruler
i'm planning to pack myself in a suitcase
and
take
a
trip
to
zanzibar
or
timbuktu
or
someplace i won't easily be found
and i'll stop sucking my thumb
and i'll stop wetting my bed

and i'll stop stealing
my brother and sister's cookies
and i'll stop behaving
like
an
out of control
top
smashing
into
everything
correcting all the wrongs
that would have made
my mommy and daddy
love
me
anyway
my best friend billy
told me
someday i'll grow up to be somebody important
like those
cool guys on the corner
talking on cell phones
slapping fives
never going to day jobs
but always taking taxis everywhere
and
wearing
the
hippest
threads
and
jewelry
and when i'm rich as any rockefeller
i'll push my parents' doorbell
and
reintroduce myself to their ordinary lives
and
they'll
say

come on in
and
have a hamburger and a coca cola
and
put your feet up on that sofa
and
you know you were right
about your sister
she's smelly
and
your older brother's creepy
and
sticks dead snakes
in his dresser drawer
just like you told us
so we crown you
prince
of
112 worth street
brooklyn
new york
u
s
o
f
a

Bruce Weber

the trunk under the bed

jackie has no survivors except this trunk. let's bust it open with a crowbar, let's rip apart it's rusty hinges, let's discover why jackie turned his back on its contents, dodging its shadows like pandora was sleeping inside its contours, let's stab it with a pitchfork, attach some high explosives to its padlock, shoot it full of bullets, so we can ponder the meaning of that 12 inch nightstick, that almost empty tub of vaseline, that box of amyl nitrate, that enema bag marked with his initials, that sheaf of photographs of cemetery stones held together by a weary rubber band, let's sniff the black leather garments, let's turn the pages of his sadomasochistic magazines, let's look at every snapshot of his boyfriends, let's read every love letter, now that jackie's passed on to his reward at the age of forty seven, let's blow that trunk open, so we can come to some feeble understanding of who jackie was before he married peggy sue.

who's revolution?

for Jushi

who's revolution? your revolution? max's revolution? glady's revolution? huh? what? revo. revo. lution. woodstock? berlin? bratislava? birmingham? let's have a revolution! let's make a revolution? come on paint a pretty picture of a revolution. a revolution less guns or tanks or missiles or bombs or blood. greaseless. stainless. viewed only on video tape. archived for later playback on tv after the scars have healed. after the dead've risen up like peasants in chiang province minus crucified holes in their hands. a revolution without theorists sticking their middle finger out at generals and their double agent mistresses. revo / revo / lution. that went well together. like trotsky diego rivera and his painter wife frida kahlo. raising fists to the sky. fighting for the proletariat. yes trotsky rivera and frida started a mexican revolution. in paint. in body fluids. in revolutionary phrases. revo. revo. o pretty little revo. pretty little revolution.

Bruce Weber

o my god everything's melting

o
my
god
o
my
god
everything's
melting
o
my
god
everything's
melting
that clock
that big clock
that big clock on that skyscraper's melting
that big clock on that skyscraper's melting like fondue
like fondue
o
my
god
the city's turning into a puddle
a vast puddle of ooze
o
my
god
i'm slipping
i'm slipping
yuch
oh
it's
disgusting
everything's melting
and it's coming after me
like a monster emerging from the sea
in a 1950s horror movie
symbolizing the atom bombing of
hiroshima and nagasaki

o
my
god
they're gonna drop
another atomic bomb on it
they're gonna blow it to kingdom come
they're gonna destroy it
without a second's thought
obliterate it
without blinking
o
my
god
everything's melting
everything's melting
everything's melting
o
my
god
o
my
god
i'm sliding down broadway
i'm sliding down broadway
into
the
harbor
into
the
harbor
watch out for that tugboat
that cute little tugboat
and
the
ferry
the staten island ferry
watch
out
for

Bruce Weber

the
fucking
staten
island
ferry
o
my
god
hand me a beach towel
yuch
how
r
e
v
o
l
t
i
n
g
o
my
god
the world's completely liquid
the world's completely liquid
o
my
god
everything's
melting
everything's
m
e
l
t
i
n
g

diary entry 1001

received a bizarre e-mail last night. something about my participation in a three ring plot to atomize the island of manhattan. strange coded words alluding to kamikaze actions. must have been sent to me by accident. don't remember signing up for such covert behavior with a foreign terrorist organization. unless it was during my infamous black out period last month when everything about my life seemed to evaporate in thin air. that frightened family and friends into demanding i undergo a full medical checkup which came up without an explanation for why i feel impelled to participate in a terrorist plot. something is pulling me toward the keyboard to answer in the affirmative and fulfill my obligation to assist in releasing catastrophic bomb in air. feels like the "right thing" to do. feel bad about this but helpless to throw up hands and say no. tomorrow is d day. 9 o'clock sharp.

Bruce Weber

what did sally saw?

what
did
sally
saw
that
made
her
jump
out
of
her
scrawny
body?
what
did
sally
saw
running
across
the
weed
infested
garden?
what
did
sally
saw
that
scared
her
up
a
tree
house?
what
did
sally
saw

crouched
in
a
corner
signaling
for
her
to
come
feed
it?
what
caused
her
to
pack
up
her
coloring
book
her
crayons
her
favorite
dolly
franny
and
crawl
into
a
hole
left
in
the
earth
by
a
possum?
what

Bruce Weber

did
sally
saw
that
crossed
her
path
one
summer
day
and
caused
her
to
become
a
turnip
that
made
her
close
up
like
a
lid
on
a
coffin
that
whizzed
across
the
periphery
of
her
senses
like
a
five

alarm
fire?
what
did
sally
saw
that
made
her
apologize
to
god
for
only
being
seven?

Bruce Weber

diary entries

jan 11

saw spud at ice rink last night. told me randy and kren split up. not surprised. kren was cheating on him with every guy in her computer class. randy wasn't a perfect gentleman either. i saw him having sex with that nurse katrina out in the tool shed a couple of months ago. nice looking lady that katrina.

jan 12

told izzy i was having trouble with lorette. he slapped me so hard on the back i thought i'd puke. seems lorette and izzy go way back. can't trust anyone with my feelings. it always hurts.

jan 13

looked for god in the details today. after attending emerson lecture at the university. seems like ralph was a pretty good guy. not as poetic as his protégé thoreau though. fell asleep a couple of times. woke up and pulled out my magnifying glass and started inspecting things "up close".

jan 14

elmer came over tonight. we shared a bottle of beaujolais and he confessed to stealing money from the petty cash box at his office. told him to put it back.

jan 15

laughed a lot today. especially when peter called and told me about his date with angelina. they went to an italian place on carmine street and witnessed a mob hit. pretty funny.

jan 16

glanced around at work today and realized i hated everyone.

jan 17

spent lunch hour pouring over the wants ads. may look into the position of truant officer at belvedere high.

jan 18

ran into paddy flanagan on 14th street. paddy was loaded and it wasn't 10 am yet. sad. muy triste. that's french for very sad.

jan 19

sally has a great butt. she really does.

jan 20

joined the choral group for a rehearsal of bach's oratorio in g major. what a hoot when linda sorvalini broke the glass. all of us howled like banshees.

jan 21

larry called. read me his new poem about cows:
         moo moo.
         the cow said.
         moo moo moo.
         the cow said.
thought it showed promise.

jan 22

enjoyed the art show on bedford avenue. seems the guy has an interest in bright colors and peculiar angles. the way light shimmers in corners. the sudden burst of a blue or pink or orange. the installation whispered to me. circling my soul like a halo. a sudden instigation of beauty. of beauty for its own sake. no hidden agendas. no surprising junctures between what we know and what we can only imagine. interesting. very interesting. so interesting i wanted to sleep there. reclining my head on the color lavender. the lavender that leaned like a delicate ballerina. across from the tiptoeing emerald green. that played paddy cake paddy cake with the oceanic gray.

suddenly it was as if i was surrounded by a wall of waves breaking on shore. the whoosh and tumble of a room that slept in my arms like a playful child. a playful child dreaming of a divine light. a divine light lifting us all up on its shoulders. lifting us up on its shoulders so we can see the beauty of the world.

hey ms. kemble

hey
ms. kemble
don't shy away
when i ask for another renewal
of the kama sutra
don't pretend
i'm not making you stir
underneath
your unfashionable clothing
don't pretend
my animal magnetism's
not popping open
the metal button's
on your blouse
please
ms. kemble
allow my dark eyes
to penetrate
your cool behavior
whenever i request
the key
to the men's room
i ain't asking you
to show me
what you got
under that matronly outfit
you bought at sears roebuck
or
put every book
on special reserve
about the sexual behavior
of the ancient romans
i'd just like
to take you out
for a wild night
of ballroom dancing
kicking off our shoes
and doing

Bruce Weber

the fox trot
the cha cha
and a couple of turns
of the tarantella
i won't get out of line
i'll keep my dancer's distance
never getting close enough
to nibble on your earlobe
never letting my hand
slide down your waist
to your pretty little bottom
i won't whisper any sex come on's
when the big band's
heating up their chops
with take the a train
hey
ms. kemble
i'm your most devoted
member of the public
so
stop giving me
the cold shoulder
whenever i ask directions
to adult fiction
loosen the hair from your bun
remove your thick glasses
take that uptight pout off your lips
and pucker me up
with a modicum
of warmth
and consideration
because
i'm
working
on
my
ph.d.
in
carnal
knowledge

This Story Is Cooking

This story is cooking.
At 360 degrees.
In an hour it will be finished.
Before then I'd like to introduce you to the spices.
The salt.
The hot pepper.
The cardomon.
The bay leaf.
Sniff deeply.
Do not be afraid of sneezing.
Sneezing is a form of catharsis.
A freeing of inner demons.
A letting go of the monkey bars.
A form of art practiced in Turkey.
Now let me show you the recipe.
Turn to page 567.
The instructions are found
In the labyrinthian folds
Of a mantra
Painted by a cheerful old seer
Named Charlie Foo.
He's my adopted uncle.
I'm his imaginary nephew.
Sometimes he hits me over the head
When I confuse
Rosemary for thyme
Or
Sage for licorice root
And laughs like a storm coming into town
At a 170 degree angle
Knocking off the heads
Of old trees
Like a psychopath with a temperamental buzzsaw.
I love my uncle
Even when he hits me
For choosing the incorrect ingredient
But this story is almost cooked
And I'm certain it's perfect.

Bruce Weber

I wish life could be like that.
A perfect hue on the outside
And tender on the inside.
Everyone quoting
The Diamond Sutra
Wearing silk robes
Dancing on the head of an invisible pin
Visible only to the most excellent chefs.
The ones capable of understanding
The meaning of pebbles
In a universe crowded by
Bad drivers
Honking horns.

How To Stay In Love With Your Girlfriend
Who Has Cats
When You're Allergic

1. Never fail to remember where you rate in the feline equation.

2. Never threaten her with a *them* or *me* proposal.

3. Never admit you're wheezing when one of the cats just happens to be sitting on your head.

4. Humor her when she asks you to hold each cat for as long as it takes for them to stop hissing.

5. Pretend she's referring to orphans in the wilds of Siberia.

6. Smile when she announces the cats will be joining the two of you for a candlelight supper.

7. Never question the difference between human and animal love.

Bruce Weber

when i was an ant

when i was an ant
to my brother's rhinoceros
the wind kicked its sails through our boat
like it was the coming of the savior
i spooned enough honey into my mouth for celebration
enough to save the school of sparrows that nested
under the eave of the front window
no matter what the strength of the season
i could stomach any kind of bird call
it didn't matter if i was asleep and dreaming
cause when i spoke children would stop riding their bicycles
and sit close enough up to my mouth
to listen to every whippoorwhill call or woodpecker peck
i could create in repetition of what i heard
i was a regular menagerie of sounds
manmade and human
i could replicate the whirr under the earth of a big electronic snake
searching for the relics of the dead
or tumble like a roller coaster in the throes
of a speed of light ride
the intuition i was born with
rode around in my back pocket
like a map or handkerchief or wallet
coughing up any bugs too small to surrender to my swallow
i'd crouch like a sniper
pretending to take down anything that had an inkling
to change the way things was
that's when pappa died
and we ran around the porch
circling it like indians
not understanding
there would be no more horseback rides
on his shoulders
sometimes you can't measure
what you once had
you have
to hold it up to your nose
and sniff deeply

the world

1.

the world looks larger now. somehow everything is the scale of the titantic. underwater. ruined. rusted. oblivious to fish or fowl. the world the size of a beach ball to an infant. rounder than a mother's nipple. more plentiful than spit in the throat of the flu patient. an endless exchange of air between the busboy and the elderly heart attack victim at the restaurant. the world skipping. holding hands. innocent as springtime. carried away in heart song. looming among the vidalia onions. picking lowee's pocket at the bus station. the world cozying up to the mafioso. to the hired assassin. to the judgmental poet striking everyone down with a sneer and a shot of bourbon. the world humming to itself in the shower. washing behind its ears. trimming its whiskers. slapping itself awake with a handful of shaving lotion. the world the size of mount kilimanjaro. the rockies. the mountain ranges of cézanne's imagination.

2.

the world shrinking like a violet. disappearing in purple. in dark blue. in blackness. the world vanishing behind a hard curve. an embarrassing query. a letter from the government pointing a tall finger. the world absent. missing. out to lunch. dreaming of small intangible things. the air occupying that chair. the unmistakable curve of a lover's arm. the juxtaposition of light and dark in a poem by satan. the world hedging its bets at the window of life. putting two dollars down on a hundred to one shot. sneaking out the back door and escaping the long nose of the law. the world hissing like a python. anticipating the distance of its lunge like an olympic diver. breaking its fall with a chorus of hallelujah's and a prayer and a sob. the world escaping like air from the pricked balloon. whooshing out. outdistancing the good intentions of god.

3.

the world is simple. a box. four walls. sometimes sky. everything simpatico. everything fragrant. plentiful. green. the world a child's drawing. flat. free of science. spontaneous. elemental. the world napping under the apple tree heavy with sweetness. running in a field of wild flowers with dick and jane. with beautiful dick and jane. the world happy. smiling. comfortably full. napping on the front porch. dreaming the afternoon away.

Bruce Weber

situations

for Miriam Stanley

situations are sometimes like this.
the voice in the other room.
the consistent hum of the refrigerator.
animals talking to the air
out of sorts with their fur.
on the tv
a man swings
and
a ball flies
a thousand miles away
where women cover their heads in prayer to allah
and jews sweep away anger with a helpless broom.
situations are like this sometimes
in the dark apartment
where a harp plays
on a scratched record
looking for the sun.
in these situations
someone peels a scab away.
someone runs up a flagpole.
there is an electricity here
that runs in and out of situations.
someone wiping their mouth of moisture.
watching the gerbil climb
on the turning wheel
in the ever present dark.

what sheila brought home

the aromatic bird.
the yowling rock.
the implacable worm.
the tenacious hook.
these are the things that weigh sheila down.
the heebee jeebees in the telephone wire.
the blank stare from the painted wall.
these hard knocks
swell sheila's v i s i s i t u d e s
so
sheila whistles
god bless america.
sheila salutes herself
in the mirror.
sheila defies explanations
bringing home
cute things
that explode in the night.
the yellow pocket watch.
the red wagon.
the white broach.
the green assumption.
stammer like shivering children.
clasp their hands together in prayer.
slip into the ripe night of love
and
cling
together
like
snails
or
turtles
or
insects.
the lingering rain.
the secretive statue.
the frantic kiss.

Bruce Weber

are you confused about the nature of this poem?

are you confused about the nature of this poem? no? then why are you acting so mindless? what's robbed your intelligence of its sense of fairplay? isn't there anything that can be done to remind you life's just a gay old time my friend? would hypnosis work? how about short declarative sentences? dynamite? prayer? a sexual escapade starring the model of your choice? try door a? try door b? try door c? are you feeling fragmented? are parts of you spread like a tango dancer's fan across the terrain of the ballroom? is this poem twisting you in the wind like a tree nestled in the arms of an angry god? can you take a moment, descend on one knee, and remain silent for a minute of unspoken devotion to god's invisibility – like the ghost moving back and forth across the floor of my apartment – restless, wobbling, intoxicated? and can i paint you someone no longer listless, faded, vacant? someone pink or evergreen or sky blue and polka dotted? someone with the creamy white skin of a perfect human specimen painted by ingres? can this poem turn into a tall tale in a novel by twain or an exaggerated passage in dickens inspiring your mouth to open like a capitol o? hey did i just motivate some dust to fall off your shoulders with a thump? did i just shake the core of your world like an apple orchard? or are you simply coming apart like a 3rd century b.c. greek vase tipped over at the metropolitan museum by a spunky four year old?

there's a dark black band over this poem

there's a dark black band over this poem. maybe it's being worn by the mourners of all the poets who died this week. like the chilean who lived in exile because he couldn't stomach any form of civilian mutilation or the poet with the southern accent who understood that the secret ingredient in the best plate of chitlins was love. no matter how many times you or i scratch our head the dark black band ain't going nowhere. it's like the statue of a civil war soldier in the town square always standing upright. always young and limber for patriotic principles. always prepared for any battle threatening the republic. like a simile that pours through our fingers. like the water from a stream after a long hike through gettysburg in search of the shadows left behind by a great great grandfather who died with a copy of leaves of grass tucked in his back pocket. though i ain't no praying man i'm getting on my knees now and saying a little something for all the poets who passed away this week into the here ever after.

Appendix

Alphabetical Index

Alphabetical Index continued...

•

ROGUE SCHOLARS
Press

For book ordering information or a price quote for our
book design services, go to:

http://www.roguepress.com

For General Information, e-mail:

info@roguescholars.com

Editor-In-Chief, C. D. Johnson:

editor-in-chief@roguescholars.com

Senior/Submissions editor, Miriam Stanley:

miriam@roguescholars.com

If you wish to submit material to Rogue Scholars Press,
please read our guidelines first.

For complete and up-to-date guidelines, go to:

http://www.roguescholars.com/submit

•

Not To Be
Believed
MIRIAM STANLEY

Journey To The
Center Of My Mind
PATRICIA CARRAGON
Publisher: Carragon

Cat Breath
**A TWO-HEADED
KITTY
ANTHOLOGY**

Club Fascistland
**KEVIN BRINK
NIELSEN**
Publisher: Authorhouse

Awakened
**MADELINE
ARTENBERG**
and
IRIS N. SCHWARTZ

Lazarus
JEAN LEHRMAN

For Better Or
Verse
TOM GUARNERA

Out Of And Into
The Fray
EUGENE RING
Publisher: Ring

Get Over It
MIRIAM STANLEY

**Other publications from
Rogue Scholars Press
and our affiliates**

**To order, go to:
www.roguepress.com**

Printed in the United States
220037BV00001B/2/P

9 780977 155095